This book contains three long stories and knead to read a part of it every day for your child before bed

The story of
Ali Baba and
the Forty
Thieves

The story of Ali Baba and the forty thieves is one of the beautiful traditional tales, which is loved by adults and children, and even on his feet the abundant amount of cinema directors, due to cinematic works on the novel of Ali Baba and the forty thieves.

The story's activities: The activities of the novel take place in Baghdad in the Abbasid era, and it is said that there were two older brother brothers called Qasim and the younger one called Ali Baba, they lived with their father, the rich seller, and after their father was killed, he left them with big money, abundant funds and several lands.

However, Qasim, the first brother, seized all of his father's money due to his greed and greed, and left Ali Baba poor and even treated him poorly. Ali Baba worked a woodcutter in the woods, to provide himself with daily nutrition.

He used to go out to work in the woods, rip and inspect the timber daily from the morning until the evening, then return to the city to sell firewood, and get the wealth to buy food for his family.

Ali Baba discovers the cave of treasures: One day, while Ali Baba worked in the woods, he heard a faint voice from behind the mountainous region, Ali Baba void the effort, and hid behind a large tree and aspired to the sound, and he found 40 horsemen standing against a cave in the mountainous region.

Ali Baba began to continue the knights, and he found the leader of the cavalry moving forward and standing up to the cave, and raising his voice saying, "Open Sesame." And as soon as he finishes this item, he finds the door of the cave open in front of them, Ali Baba was surprised and approached to watch the matter closely.

The knights entered the cave and Ali Baba looked inside the cave, and found golden treasures at many rates. Ali Baba waited until he left the headquarters cavalry, approached and stood in the face of the cave and shouted the password, "Open sesame."

Ali Baba found the door of the cave open in front of him, so Ali Baba rushed in to enter the cave and sought to collect as many gold treasures as he could, and returned it to his home in the town.

Ali Baba tells his wife the secret of the treasure:

When Ali Baba's father treasure.
His wife asked him:
Where did he get these golden treasures?
He told her the story of the cave that he had discovered, in the mountainous region, and Ali Baba began to help his wife, counting the treasures that Ali Baba had stood on his feet.

However, if all the treasures and money could not be counted for their abundance, Ali Baba's wife suggested using a measure from his brother Qasim's house, until these treasures weigh.

The measure of measure: The wife of Ali Baba went to the wife of Qasim, and asked her to borrow a measure. However, the wife of Qasim was surprised by that requirement, and she decided to discover what Ali Baba wanted to impute when he was poor. The presence of honey in the measure and did not pay attention to it.

Ali Baba's wife refused the measure, and she began to weigh the treasures and golden coins, and upon the completion of the work he carried out the measure of the daddy to return it to his brother, except that he did not pay attention to the existence of until now the gold coins, attached to the bottom of the scale due to the presence of honey.

Qasim's wife discover the secret of the measure:
I took Qasim al-Qayyal's wife, looked at the depth and found gold coins so far, so I hurried and informed Qasim about that issue, so Qasim decided to monitor Ali Baba and find out the secret of this gold money until he discovered the location of the golden cave, which Ali Baba was going to

Qassem Detention:
On the following day, Qasim went out to the cave, stood in front of it, and shouted, "Open, sesame." And he found the door of the cave open, and he hurriedly entered the cave unless he found 40 thieves inside the cave.

Forty thieves got up to arrest Qasim, and they tried to kill him so he hurried and told them that his brother was also stealing the cave, so they cooperated with him to reach Ali Baba, who became rich, after his possession of these golden treasures.

Merci d'être venu Maid Morjana saves Ali Baba: Qasim and the forty thieves hid in the form of shop owners, and they went to the house of Ali Baba, to get rid of him and hid the thieves inside 40 large concealed, and stood on the feet of the thieves leader accompanied by Qasim to knock on the door of the house of Ali Baba, and told him that they are a number of owners of oil trade, and darkness came They want a shelter headquarters until dawn.!

Appealing to Ali Baba, his female neighbor, Morgana, to prepare food for them and welcome them, so Morgana went to prepare food for them, but she did not find oil, so Ali Baba asked her to take oil from the large cache of sellers.

As Morgana opens one of Al-Khawabi, and with her you find men with leather swords inside, Murjanah rushed and covered the crater of the Alkhabia with large stones, so that men could not go outside.

Morgana carried a big knife, she went to Ali Baba, pretended to sway and dance, approached the thief leader and stabbed him, surprised Baba, the thing his female mourjan did.

But she told him about the hidden thieves, so Ali Baba rushed, and the thieves fought a fantasy hidden in my oil, until he ordered them together, and thanked Ali Baba Morgana, for what she did in the rescue of his life and the discovery that the thieves spent.

the and

THE STORY OF THE THREE LITTLE CHICKEN

One day, there were three brothers of chicken, one of them a cook, 2 carpenters, and 3 mourners. The three siblings decided to build homes for themselves to live in.

The three siblings began to implement the house-building decree, and they began construction, the largest intended to build his house from straw, the 2 issued a decision to build his house out of wood, and the 3 issued a decision to build his house out of bricks.

Their 3 brothers stated to them: My brothers, straw and wood are not suitable for building houses, as straw may be destroyed by wind, and wood may be affected by rain, thunder and lightning.

But they did not hear him and both of them decided to start building their house alone, without the help of one of them, and they started construction.

Their 3 brothers had compassion on their buildings, they are very weak, and will be affected by the weakest effects such as heat, rain, wind, thunder and lightning, and any movement that may take place in weather conditions will affect their homes and may completely destroy them, and also not protect them from the fox.

After the construction, the older brother completed the construction of his straw house on the largest day of construction, and he kept laughing, saying:

- I finished building my house, I am now completely free, I am very happy .. He kept laughing loudly, and his 2 brother worked on working very quickly until he became full like him.

The next day, the 2nd brother crossed out the construction of his house, which he intended to build from wood, and he was also happy to build his house, and he also continued to laughter loudly. He lost, became free, and he will rest in the wake of that construction, which remained for 48 hours, and goes to his brothers saying:

- I am very happy, I finished building the house, it was a difficult work that lasted for two whole days, and now I will just rest, I have finished building the house, I have my own house, I own a modern house

The older brother replied: Blessed brother, I am currently resting, your house is very beautiful, but it took 48 hours for you to complete the effort, so it is a tiring work, but my house took a single day to build, so it is more superior.

Brother, the wood is harder than the straw, and I'm delighted at home.

The 3 brother entered the dialogue saying: except that the bricks are stronger, because you know very well that the wolf these days is close to us, and we must cooperate to create a solid house that the wolf cannot enter, but you did not give me your attention, I fear for you, my brothers.

Above him the elder brother replied, and the second: No, the wolf will not be able to approach our homes. We built them carefully, and the wolf will not dare touch them. He left them and did not talk to them again.

Until everyone in his house was knocking on the door of the largest chicken, he said: Who?

- My brother, I open
to me, except that
the chicken saw the
body of the wolf and
knew that it was not
his brother, so he was
afraid to open it to
eat and he said: No,
you are the wolf, I will
not open for you

And the wolf said: If
you don't open the
door for me, I'll blow
in your house and it
will be destroyed
He told him: She will
not be able.

The wolf blew up in the house, and the straw-made house fell, so the larger chicken sped out of his house and headed to his brother's 2 house, after which he knocked on the door of the second chicken.

He said: I will not open to you, wolf, we two are harder than you.
And the wolf said: If you don't open the door for me, I will blow in your house and it will be destroyed.
He told him: It will not.

The wolf blew up in the house, and the house made of wood fell, so the oldest chicken and 2 rushed out from the second hen house heading to their brother's 3 house.

Then he knocked
on the door of the
3 hen:
He said: I will not
open to you, wolf,
we are three
harder than you.
And the wolf said:
If you don't open
the door for me, I'll
blow in your house
and it will be
destroyed.
He told him: It will
not

Merci The wolf blew into the house and did not collapse, and he continued to seek to blow into it and not to collapse, and he sought to detonate it except that the house was of solid strength, because the 3 hen mastered his work, and the three siblings lived in their brother's 3 house made of bricks, because the house was solid because it was made perfect.d'être venu !

the and

The story
of the
Kings

Once upon a time, in the past, there was a large city, ruled by a great king, but the people of that city, did not grant the king to any of the kings, except for a period of only one year, and after the completion of the reign of the king, the people of that big city, They send the king to a faraway island a lot, and the goal was for the king to live in it for the rest of his life, until they nominate another king other than they want.

And once upon a time, one of the kings had assumed the rule of that big city, and when his rule ended, and his ownership of the country, and the reaction of the people of the city, was very different from previous times, as they were taking the clothes of the king, and not allowing him, to remain retained It out.

But that time, they allowed that king, to remain dressed in the king's precious clothes, and circled the king throughout the whole city, and chanting together sings filled with grief and sorrow, for that great king: "Goodbye, great king, goodbye, great king."

That moment was very harsh, and extremely difficult, not only for the king, but for the people of the city, and for all their kings. The people of the city dedicated a large, and very impressive ship, until you transport the king, to the remote island, where he will complete the rest of his life.

The ship transported the king, and then returned on its way to the big city. On the way to the ship, its passengers found that another ship had sunk not long ago, and there was a young man in that ship, attached to a piece of wood, which sank in it Immediately over the water, they rescued the young man, and transported him with them to the big city, and the city people asked that young man, to be king over them for one year, but he refused, but with the insistence of the people he agreed with difficulty.

The young man knew all the rulings that were imposed on the king, and after three days, the young man asked to see the island, so when he went, he found that it was like a forest, with strange and evil animal sounds, and discovered that the corpses of kings are thrown on the ground, everywhere, so he returned to the city And he gathered one hundred workers, and made them clean the island, including what he asked them to build a marina for ships, and began to supervise them.

After they finished that, the island became a wonderful and beautiful place, the king took, spending huge amounts of money on the island, instead of clothes and city expenses, and after the year ended, the king prepared to go to the island, and he was optimistic and very happy, unlike the rest of the kings, when he was asked On the reason,

he answered that
the kings had been
preoccupied with
temporal
enjoyment with
clothes and the
city, and they did
not look to the
future as he did, as
he made the city a
paradise, so he
could live a
comfortable life in
it.

the end